PAMPHLETS ON AMERICAN WRITERS · NUMBER 91

UNIVERSITY OF MINNESOTA

John Barth

BY GERHARD JOSEPH

UNIVERSITY OF MINNESOTA PRESS · MINNEAPOLIS

Printed in the United States of America at the
Lund Press, Minneapolis

Library of Congress Catalog Card Number: 70-629877

Permission to quote from John Barth's unpublished lecture
"Mystery and Tragedy: The Two Motions of Ritual
Heroism" was granted by Mr. Barth.

PUBLISHED IN GREAT BRITAIN, INDIA, AND PAKISTAN BY THE OXFORD
UNIVERSITY PRESS, LONDON, BOMBAY, AND KARACHI, AND IN CANADA
BY THE COPP CLARK PUBLISHING CO. LIMITED, TORONTO

JOHN BARTH

GERHARD JOSEPH is an associate professor of English at Herbert H. Lehman College, City University of New York. He is the author of the book *Tennysonian Love: The Strange Diagonal* (University of Minnesota Press).

↙ *John Barth*

THE biographical surface of John Barth's life appears to be all but seamlessly academic. Born in Cambridge, Maryland, in 1930 he attended public schools, graduating from Cambridge High. After a brief stay at the Juilliard School of Music, he entered Johns Hopkins, was married in 1950, graduated with a B.A. in 1951 and an M.A. in 1952. He began teaching at Pennsylvania State University in 1953 and moved on to the State University of New York at Buffalo in 1965, where he became a writer in residence and professor of English. Barth's published fictions, that is, have developed without exception within the sheltering and/ or confining umbra of the American school. To be sure, the tiresomely repeated question of whether the academic groves have been a blessing or a curse for the American writer is — certainly in Barth's mind — beside the point. As he has noted in an interview, excellent art has always come from all sorts of backgrounds: "any kind of life at all . . . can be shown to have produced work that you admire." The university atmosphere and the profession of writer-teacher just happen to be conditions of his work, inherently neither better nor worse than conceivable alternatives.

Still, an interim account of Barth's development may as well document the truism that his continuing immersion in a self-consciously intellectual world has crucially determined his direction as a writer. While his novels are not conventionally "academic," the educational experience either as theme or all-encompassing metaphor is central to each of them. They look back vaguely to the *Bildungsroman*, for in them, as the very title of Barth's second work would suggest, Western man has come to the end of the philosophical road first explored in this eighteenth- and nineteenth-century genre. And the complex response of a tutee to his tutor or psycho-spiritual adviser is a primary confrontation in several works. This abiding interest in the metabolism of human learning finds its terminus, thus far, in the novel-long pun of *Giles Goat-Boy* wherein the hero's life in the universe is allegorized as a movement through the cosmic University.

In their local effects as well the novels allude to their seminal idea of education — and frequently education in its institutional forms. Jake Horner and Joe Morgan of *The End of the Road* are compared partially in the light of their respective progress through the Johns Hopkins Graduate School. The protagonist of *The Floating Opera*, Todd Andrews, glances back at his own Johns Hopkins education with a momentary verve that sharply contrasts with his habitual torpor. A phlegmatic soul rarely given to enthusiasm for anything, he can throw off a tribute to "the men, the professors, the fine independent minds of Johns Hopkins" and their disinterested search for wisdom. For better or worse, Barth is the kind of novelist that one might expect to come out of the Johns Hopkins graduate program, with its rigorous scholarly standards and history of ideas orientation. Certainly, while he somewhat disingenuously denies any philosophical competence ("I don't know anything about philosophy. I've never studied it, much less learned it"), the character conflicts of his novels are grounded less in temperamental differences than in philosophical debates of a rather abstruse sort. Sexual encounters between men and women occur frequently enough, but there is usually something tentative and halfhearted about the participation in them by semi-impotent or virginal protagonists. Barth's real narrative passion is reserved for voracious clashes of mind. His heroes, as Todd Andrews says of himself, tend "to attribute to abstract ideas a life-or-death significance," while his women are hollow, accommodating disciples in whom the men deposit the seed of not so much a sexual as a philosophical obsession. The passionate struggle of intellectually well-entrenched male opponents who are inverted "doubles" of each other and whose ideas meet upon the essentially empty and undefended battlefield of a woman is most fully elaborated in *End of the Road*, but this paradigm serves either as the structural base or as the architectural ornament of Barth's other novels.

Such skirmishes of mind are rather firmly grounded, at least at first, in regional verisimilitude. For Barth is in his early work an accurate comic observer of Dorcester County, Maryland, and his books abound in local circumstance, character, and mores. *Floating Opera*, *End of the Road*, "Landscape: The Eastern Shore," and the "Ambrose" stories of *Lost in the Funhouse* are filled with the details of Maryland law and legal maneuvering, with the dry, hard texture of Maryland beaten biscuit, with evocations of Ocean City boardwalk and Baltimore social life. Barth's intimate knowledge of Maryland history, at any rate of the devious intrigues of the Chesapeake tidewater country in the seventeenth century, emerges with a hyperbolic exhaustiveness in *Sot-Weed Factor*. But the regional and historical verisimilitude of the first three novels merely supplies a base — and an increasingly mock one — for moral allegory and mythic flight. As Barth's interest in the ancient archetypes of his early "seekers" became more sharply focused, he began in his later work to trace the pattern of the hero's education into selfhood ("that hero business") with an increasingly experimental and self-reductive playfulness. In *Giles* the pretense of social and historical, if not entirely psychological, realism is altogether eschewed, as Barth follows the mythic configurations of the Western hero with a purposeful directness and artificiality.

This flight from realism to parodic fable turns out to be a flight from time to timelessness. The credible contemporary reality of *Floating Opera* and *End of the Road* gives way in *Sot-Weed Fac-*

tor to a seventeenth-century setting, a burlesque upon the Maryland past which employs the historian's questionable "facts" in the service of the novelist's quasi-historical, universal fable. And while the goat-boy's *Heldensleben* plays itself out against the background of crudely disguised Cold War politics, the political allegory is so patently subordinate to its pan-historical archetype (as is the life of the goat-boy) that the University of *Giles* with its multiple historical and cultural cross-references encompasses all times.

The irreversible quality of Barth's drift from time-bound realism to timeless fable is encapsulated in his comments, during an interview, on experiments in the novel by the French: ". . . the *nouveau roman* isn't just my cup of tea. They're all fighting Balzac, as I understand it, and I guess some of *us* are mad at Flaubert instead, in a friendly way. From what I know of Robbe-Grillet and his pals, their aesthetic is finally a more up-to-date kind of psychological realism: a higher fi to human consciousness and unconsciousness. Well, that's nice. A different way to come to terms with the discrepancy between art and the Real Thing is to *affirm* the artificial element in art (you can't get rid of it anyhow), and make the artifice part of your point instead of working for higher and higher fi with a lot of literary woofers and tweeters. That would be my way. Scheherazade's my *avant-gardiste*."

Like Scheherazade's tales, the thematic stuff of Barth's preposterous fictions does not undergo enormous change from work to work. His heroes try to find a philosophical justification for life, search for values and a basis for action in a relativistic cosmos, concern themselves with the possibilities of philosophical freedom and with the question of whether character and external reality are stable or floating phenomena. His novels, in other words, abound in many of the conceptual chestnuts of a post-Frazerian, Freudian, Wittgensteinian, Jungian, Sartrian world, and they usually parody

8

the formulations of such classical modernists. What distinguishes Barth's habitual tone is a sophisticated, self-mocking awareness of how late in the game he has come to such "inquiries" (Todd Andrews' word) and how burned out the techniques of social and psychological realism are for handling them. Understanding that "God wasn't too bad a novelist, except he was a Realist," Barth has progressively committed himself to dreaming up "fictional" (in Jorge Luis Borges' sense of the word) alternatives to the cosmos, to reinventing the whole history of the world (in *Giles*, the world's sacred computer tape) with a coherence that the Real Thing lacks.

The Floating Opera, the first novel of a remarkably finished craftsman (or as the early Barth might prefer, boatwright), seemed to many of its early reviewers a comedy of manners with an "existential" keel. Securely tied to its Chesapeake Bay moorings, it ripples forth the widening circles of Barth country — Cambridge and the Choptank River, Dorcester County, the Eastern Shore of Maryland with its social and intellectual hub in Baltimore. The breezy accent, the eccentric but well-mannered intelligence, and the border-South financial security of the novel's protagonist bespeak a social ambience reminiscent of the Maryland that F. Scott Fitzgerald occasionally evoked in his work and of a cosmopolitan South that has more recently been Walker Percy's preserve. Todd tells his tale in the first person — of Barth's novels, only *Sot-Weed Factor* does not employ this habitual perspective which allows for progressively deepening experimentation with the sounds of the human, quasi-authorial voice.

The narrative's temporal dislocations are the accomplished tour de force of an author who wishes to involve his audience as demandingly as possible in the protagonist's self-discoveries, but Barth handles such a staple device of the modern novel with a virtuosity that suggests complete mastery of the convention. What was tech-

9

nically revolutionary in Conrad or Faulkner, so this first novel implies, is the veriest commonplace of the contemporary writer. Todd at age 54 tells the story in 1954 from which perspective he zigzags up to, through, and away from a watershed day of his life in 1937. His tongue-in-cheek excuse for the rudderless vessel his narrative resembles — a mélange of foreshadowings, anecdotal digressions, retrospective glances — is that he is something of a novice and bungler at storytelling. But we soon recognize the validity of his insistence that his method, while unsystematic, is justified by his intention.

For one thing the refracted structure is the ideal foundation for the phantasmagoric trope upon which the novel is erected. Todd enjoys spiking the reader's symbolic imagination by himself explicating heavy-handed symbols everywhere — his name (almost *Tod*, almost "death"), his ridiculous "weak heart" (clubbed fingers persistently remind him of his subacute bacteriological endocarditis, a condition that has made him live the better part of his life with the knowledge he is apt to fall down dead at any moment), and, most elaborately, "Adam's Original and Unparalleled 'Ocean-Going' Floating Opera." A tidewater country showboat with a realistic enough anchorage in the plot and in Barth's memories of his youth, the Floating Opera becomes in Todd's mind the apt correlative for his tale. In a fireworks display of his metaphorical talents he builds the fancy of such a boat drifting up and down the river with a play going on continuously. As the viewers sit upon the banks snatching at pieces of the plot and dialogue and relying for the rest on their imagination or on that of their more attentive neighbors, the boat moves back and forth before their single limited perspective. Since that is how much of life works, that's how Todd's vagrant narrative, a "philosophical minstrel show," will work as well. Todd's Floating Opera within Barth's *Floating Opera* achieves a further permutation in Todd's unsuccessful attempts at literal boat-building, and the replicating device is Barth's earliest handling of the *regressus in infinitum* — the refracting funhouse mirror, authorial echo chamber metaphor for existence that will become more pronounced in his later work.

Perspective, then, in life as in art is all-important in its distortion of event, and the 1954 perspective of a 54-year-old child of his century randomly blurs a profound division in Todd. His narrative focuses upon the day when he "changed his mind," when after having decided to commit suicide he decides, after a botched effort, not to. But the resonant phrase refers more importantly to a radical alteration of personality. For there are "two" Todds: the pre-1937 one, who if "almost dead" is also half-alive, sexually active, and apparently master of his life, gives way to a post-1937 Todd rendered moribund by a philosophical nihilism and sexually undone. The absolute force of this change is indicated by its dating. In the novel's 1956 edition Todd mentions repeatedly that the "change of mind" occurred on "either the 23rd or the 24th" of June 1937. The reason for this pointed vacillation becomes apparent only in the 1967 edition, where the correction to "either the 21st or the 22nd" clarifies Todd's abrupt declension from one house of the zodiac (Gemini, which ends on June 21) to another (Cancer, which begins on June 22).

The pre-1937 Todd was not precisely a robust innocent: he had passed through several stages, given himself over to several tepid commitments, and engaged in his share of "halfhearted" affairs. The first significant event in Todd's life occurs at seventeen when during his earliest clumsy attempts at lovemaking he happens to look into a full-length mirror and explodes into laughter at the absurdity of human copulation. The first of many optical epiphanies in Barth's work, that laugh partially unmans Todd, for he can never thereafter take liaisons with complete seriousness. True, he does carry on an extended affair between 1932 and 1937 with Jane Mack, one that has been engineered primarily by her husband for any number of quaint motives. But though a child is born who may or may not be Todd's, he keeps a discreet emotional distance between himself and both Macks. The recognition of his and mankind's animality is embellished by a World War I experience of the single "purest and strongest emotion" of his life, a moment of unadulterated, sphincter-opening terror when during a lull in battle he discovers himself to be "a shocked, drooling animal in a mudhole." This insight receives its existential cast when a German soldier in whom he induces a terror akin to his own leaps into his mudhole. After befriending the soldier in some hours of delirious intimacy, Todd bayonets him in an act as arbitrarily gratuitous as the initial embrace. And finally there is the inexplicable suicide of his father that becomes the subject of a systematic, lifelong *Inquiry*. Reflecting Todd's awareness that any single act is endlessly mysterious, that if it is not "free" (causation, with Hume, being merely an inference), then its motives are tortuously complicated, this "search for the father" becomes the instrument of Todd's attempted comprehension of the son.

Such a tissue of experiences has made for a passionless and stunted, but nevertheless comfortable, life up to 1937. Having drifted into law, as much as anything to please his lawyer father, Todd is by his own admission and as his narrative illustrates "perhaps the best lawyer on the Eastern Shore" precisely because of his detachment and his hypersensitivity to life's contingent nature. Aware of the whimsicality of choice behind the illusion of conscious intention, he takes an expert, disinterested pleasure in the law's labyrinthine and prescribed arbitrariness. He has some aged cronies in the Dorset Hotel where he lives, some friends in Cambridge proper, and his mistress of five years' standing. What bursts his unenthusiastic metaphysical ease on the night of the 20th is Jane Mack's chance remark concerning the ugliness of his clubbed hands in an otherwise admirable body. The remark triggers a sudden overwhelming nausea at the realization that his whole life has been governed by the brute, animal fact of his heart. His despair at the certainty that *"there is no way to master the fact with which I live"* makes him decide upon the "stance to end all stances," suicide.

The inescapable presence of those ugly fingers, Whitehead's sheer "withness of the body," suddenly releases a pent-up self-loathing and hatred of the too too sullied flesh of this world that, beneath Todd's congenial voice, is virtually Manichaean in its intensity. Barth's sexual and excremental humor, which in *Sot-Weed Factor* will approach the savage playfulness of a Swift, has precisely such a gnostic base. To be sure, the artificial constructs of Todd's mind conceal much of this. He makes a good deal of the "philosophical grounds" for his suicide: the discovery that his successive intellectual positions — those of rake, saint, and finally cynic — have been so many masks he has accidentally exchanged for one another and the syllogistic conclusion of the *Inquiry* that nothing, not even life itself, has any intrinsic "value." But Todd's — and Barth's — rudimentary, derivative ideas merely paper over what is most powerful in the book — the comically controlled revulsion against man, the riotously copulating Caliban, the drooling animal with twisted fingers in his mudhole.

The all-inclusiveness of Todd's naysaying determines the form of his suicide attempt — the blowing up of the Floating Opera during a performance at which seven hundred townspeople including the Macks, his possible daughter, and most of the novel's other characters are present. (In the 1956 edition Barth's publisher insisted as a condition of publication that he tone down such monstrous callousness by having Todd attempt only single suicide.) The performance itself is a climactic extravaganza. A vaudeville-paced, disjunctive, surrealistic mime of Todd's own mental peregrinations, it begins with a recitation of Hamlet's "To be or not to be" soliloquy and ends with a GREAT STEAMBOAT EXPLOSION (the Armageddon point of which is entirely clear only in the "original" 1967 conclusion). When for some accidental reason or other the real explosion does not come off, Todd refuses to try again. Why bother? If there's no final reason for living, there is no reason for dying either — *nothing* finally makes any difference. Such a retreat into the clouds of ersatz abstraction represents, it seems to me, a final failure of nerve before the "fact with which we live," for the blasé nihilism of the 54-year-old Todd seems no less of a mask than the earlier ones he has discarded. And this ultimate flinching is of course Barth's as much as Todd's (the later Barth comes to make a virtue of the necessity that his characters are funhouse mirror images of an author-protagonist), for we are meant to take with complete seriousness the terms of Todd's intellectual journey.

A lugubrious concentration upon Todd, however, does a limited justice to the novel. It ignores the fascinating minor characters and the various tales within a tale which enliven his journey — Mister Haecker's parallel struggle with the Hamlet question; Harrison Mack Senior's seventeen wills and the pickle jars filled with his excrement that become the focus of one of Todd's typical, meticulously described cases; Todd's arbitrary gift of the $5000 his father had left him to Colonel Morton, the town's richest man, and Morton's frenzied attempts to come to terms with the puzzling gift. Todd's Floating Opera — like all of Barth's works, whatever their weakness — is indeed "fraught with curiosities, melodrama, spectacle, instruction, and entertainment." But the very furiousness of invention and Todd's casual unwillingness to order the narrative swirl create a solipsistic effect. None of the characters as creations have the immediacy of the narrator's isolated voice — they are primarily part of the lonely spectacle we are asked to view from the shore; their distancing suggests movement toward an autistic cul de sac by a speaker too torpid to shun that oblivion.

Still, the end of Todd's intellectual road has not quite been reached by novel's end. The "happy ending" (words included in the title for the final chapter of the 1956, but not the 1967, edition) is in part the recovery of Mister Haecker from *his* suicide attempt and in part Todd's upbeat realization that if values are only relative, there are relative values by which one can live. The originally intended ending that Barth restored in the second edition is hardly so sanguine. Mister Haecker does indeed recover from the suicide attempt, but unlike Todd, he tries a second time and succeeds. Furthermore, Todd puts the consolation of the "happy ending" offhandedly into the form of a question rather than a delighted assertion: "I considered too whether, in the real absence of absolutes, values less than absolute mightn't be regarded as in no way inferior and even be lived by. But that's another inquiry, and another story."

The End of the Road, written in the last three months of 1955 after *The Floating Opera* had been written in the first three months of the year, is precisely that inquiry, that story. Structurally the tightest and technically the least flamboyant of Barth's works, this last leg of Barth's serious-minded youthful journey ("I thought I had invented nihilism in 1953") focuses in relatively chronological, uncharacteristically undigressive fashion upon a *ménage à trois* agreed to by the husband, a situation that had been only one of the many whizbang "curiosities" of *Floating Opera*. Whereas Todd Andrews had been a spectator to a floating reality that refused to accentuate any single dramatic antagonist, *End of the Road* transforms the "chameleon-like," lightweight Harrison Mack of the earlier work into Joe Morgan, a fanatical ideologue whose philosophical wrestling match with Jacob Horner (a refurbished Todd) ends disastrously. Instead of a sequential single life (blurred slightly by a rambling, temporal dislocation) wherein Todd Andrews is "split," as it were, by his change of mind, we witness a dialectical clash between conflicting value systems embodied in two characters.

Jake Horner, the modern rationalizer in his corner, provides a generic name for Hamlet's disease to which Todd had succumbed — *cosmopsis*, the cosmic view of things which makes for emotional hollowness and intellectual hypertrophy. The earlier novel has described Todd's evolution into the condition; this presents us with the tendency toward cosmopsis as a given of Horner's temperament. Jake is on the one hand inclined to "weatherlessness," feelings of utter nonexistence when the certainty of an essential "I" completely disappears; on the other he is agonizingly self-conscious and can usually observe himself thinking, can spot the limits of every intellectual way station he inhabits and therefore shifts from one contradictory position to another with purposeless fluidity. The price of this modern intelligence is the physical immobility into which he periodically falls. During one such bout in the Baltimore railroad station he is taken in tow by a Negro doctor —part quack, prophet, psychoanalyst ("Father Divine, Sister Kenny, and Bernarr MacFadden combined") — a vaguely threatening figure who materializes from the same numinous cosmos out of which Jacob R. Adam brought his Floating Opera to its solid moorings in Cambridge. With his preternatural understanding of Jake's disease the Doctor proceeds to put him through a series of baroque, increasingly sophisticated therapies to teach him how to choose. One such ploy, the teaching of prescriptive (*not* descriptive, the Doctor insists) grammar with is codified rigidity, becomes the extension of Todd's legal career; the conscious manipulation of "masks" that the Doctor advises at a later stage in the treatment transforms into a cure — a "Mythotherapy" remarkably like Baron de Clappique's "Mythomania" in André Malraux's *Man's Fate* — what had in *Floating Opera* been the disease itself.

If Jake's inability to choose echoes Todd's awareness that in a world devoid of absolutes nothing has intrinsic value, the Joe Morgan whom he meets during a job interview at Wicomico State Teachers College answers affirmatively the question introduced in the last paragraph of *Floating Opera* of whether man can arbitrarily set up some less than absolute value and live by it. Where Jake wanders tolerantly among equally random commitments, Joe insists that man can create his own essence by transforming a single relative value into the "subjective equivalent of an absolute." The two characters are drawn to each other precisely because their complementary minds, each initially impressive in its own erratic way, branch off from the same acceptance of modern relativism. But, having deified intellectual clarity and order, Joe lives his credo that "a man can act coherently; he can act in ways that he can explain, if he wants to." While Horner's lassitude provides him with no good reason to complete his M.A. at Johns Hopkins, a robust, vital Morgan plugs steadily away at an "odd, brilliant" thesis on the saving roles of innocence and energy in American history.

Indeed, there is a hint of an international theme in the thoroughgoing opposition of the two characters. The ancient heritage of Jake's suffering is suggested by the bust of Laocoön he carries with him from rented room to rented room, a figure whose unfocused grimace of abstract, noncommittal anguish is the archetype of Horner's own sense of a meaninglessness that is ageless. During periods of paralysis Jake's eyes take on the blank gaze that the German archaeologist Winckelmann attributed to the classical gods: he rocks in his chair "sightless, gazing on eternity, fixed on ultimacy, and when that is the case there is no reason to do anything." In contrast, Joe's buoyancy and puritanical perfectionism (a scoutmaster, he is completely aware of but impervious to the ridicule this may occasion) are peculiarly American, as he himself bouncily insists: " 'What the hell, Jake, the more sophisticated your ethics get, the stronger you have to be to stay afloat. And when you say good-by to objective values, you really have to flex your muscles and keep your eyes open, because you're on your own. It takes *energy*: not just personal energy, but cultural energy, or you're lost. Energy's what makes the difference between American pragmatism and French existentialism — where the hell else but in America could you have a cheerful nihilism, for God's sake?' "

The third character of the triangle, Rennie Morgan, becomes the crucible within which Joe attempts to prove his ethical system. Initially attracted by her surface self-sufficiency, Joe has married Rennie because he will not have to make allowances for her as a woman. Once he has finished training this apparently independent, but actually hollow disciple, he will be able to meet her as a tough-minded Galatea whose intellect he can take seriously. When Jake enters the lives of the Morgans, Joe recognizes how "diabolically" opposed Jake really is to everything he — and presumably Rennie — believe in and he intentionally throws Rennie and Jake together as an ethical experiment. For reasons as complex as his accommodating character, Jake agrees to the role of tempting devil and proceeds to chip away at Rennie's vulnerable belief in her "God's" coherence and solidity of personality.

The key blow is struck one evening when Jake challenges Rennie to spy on Joe through a living-room blind. There she sees her pillar of rationalism in his scoutmaster's uniform — grimacing, saluting, and curtseying before a mirror; making animal sounds; and then while sitting at the table where he does reading for his dissertation, simultaneously picking his nose and masturbating. The horns that Jake puts to Joe's head a few nights later seem inevitable after such a revelation, though the actual bedding down with Rennie, as Jake describes it, is initiated by neither and just "happens." When Rennie in a paroxysm of guilt and self-recrimination tells Joe what she has done, he adheres to the strait of reason with a tenacity that becomes more and more monstrous. The relentless testing that Rennie undergoes as Joe makes her return again and again to Jake's apartment in order to face up squarely to the "cause" for the betrayal transforms her into a modern-day Grisilde sacrificed upon the altar of reason rather than upon that of some medieval virtue. The obsessive talk, the microscopic probing, the scurry from one earnest conversation to another among the three characters become grotesquely comic, as Joe and Rennie pursue their analytic search and Jake insists upon the mystery of any human action wherein so many unconscious elements are involved.

It is precisely here that the novel reveals a serious weakness. Structurally, it leads up to and away from the scene at the window, although the characters all seem to mistake the adulterous act as the one that requires dissection. Jake's narration of this act goes to painful lengths to avoid any suggestion of causality, but one can easily see the "reason" why Rennie is so susceptible to a betrayal of her husband. What she learns at the window — the certainty that Joe's fierce rationalism is, if only in an unguarded moment, a mask for the Barthian fact that he like anyone else is "part chimpanzee" — weakens her belief in his authenticity. If the Morgans seek a rationale for Rennie's lapse, there it is, clear as day. Since we have but a distanced view of their introspection through what they report to a first-person narrator, we cannot be certain that the crucial nature of the window episode never occurred to them. But nothing that the Morgans say to Jake or report to him of their conversation suggests an admission to each other that Rennie's lesson at the window, not the act of adultery, ought to be the true focus of their inquiry. During a talk with Jake in which Joe does for once consider his share in the blame, he contemplates only the possibility that "for some perverse reason or other I engineered the whole affair."

Joe *never* alludes to the window scene; Rennie does at one point admit to Jake that the sight at the window "started everything," but one suspects that despite the days of tortured analysis this is not an emphasis she would have insisted upon to a "God" she feared.

Such a psychic lacuna certainly takes away from the putative "brilliance" of Joe Morgan which, of course, is suspect for other reasons; more importantly, Jake's inability to spot this suppression undermines the continuing implication of his subtlety of mind. Nor does he ever explore with requisite profundity the perversity of *his* motives for initiating Rennie into a knowledge of human complexity that night at the window. What he hides from himself is murky. It may be the homosexuality that Stanley Edgar Hyman sees as a preoccupation of all the novels; it may be that same disgust with the human body that unmanned Todd — certainly the mythotherapeutic games Jake plays with Peggy Rankin, a sexually starved, forty-year-old pickup, are a tawdry enough byplay to the central action, and he describes the abortion of Rennie, who pregnant with either Jake's or Joe's child suffocates upon her own vomit at the novel's brutal conclusion, with fascinated loathing. But despite much lip service to "human irrationality," etc., he responds with unconvincing reservations to Joe's hypothesis of a purely philosophical antagonism. The ultimate limitation of insight is once again Barth's, who suffers with his characters from a tendency to simplify an emotionally intricate, fully human confrontation into an intellectual scheme.

That a flaw in psychological structure is so glaring — one would never remark similar lapses in either *Sot-Weed Factor* or *Giles* — indicates the extent to which this novel, like *Floating Opera*, relies upon the assumptions of realism, conventions pointed up comically at the window scene and horrifyingly in the naturalistic amplitude of Rennie's abortion. But the lapse is not fatal to the novel's considerable power because the patina of realism covers with redeeming imperfection its fabular essence. Once we accept the premise of a Jake physically paralyzed by an abstract response to the world and of a Joe "who will see, face up to, and unhesitatingly act upon the extremest limits of his ideas," the larger-than-life hostility of such ideologues will inevitably lead beyond realism into philosophical fantasy. The novel's "ideas" — in part because they are embodied in such grotesques as Jake and Joe, in part because they are not as profoundly impressive as the 25-year-old Barth felt them to be — are most appropriately conveyed through parody and burlesque, a fact that may account for *Sot-Weed Factor*'s change of mode. Barth recognized something like this when in looking back upon his early novels he remarked that "I had thought I was writing about values and it turned out I was writing about innocence." That the world-weary Todd Andrews and Jake Horner are just as much naifs as Joe Morgan the novels only imperfectly convey. The stark philosophical conclusion implied in the title of the second novel therefore seems, in the light of Barth's subsequent development, sophomorically nihilistic.

Both Jake and Joe are "responsible" (a notion continually bandied about) for Rennie's disaster. Joe's mad egoism forces his wife to her death for the sake of an abstract value, while Jake resembles his Laocoön whose limbs are bound by the serpents Knowledge and Imagination that, "grown great in the fullness of time, no longer tempt but annihilate." Cursed with an excessively fertile imagination, he can never commit himself to anything or anyone. As a price for performing the abortion Jake's sinister Doctor has insisted that Jake accompany him, presumably for good, to the new location of his Remobilization Farm in Pennsylvania (a private joke, no doubt, concerning Penn State). He has in desperation agreed to the price with no intention of paying, but once Rennie is dead Jake recognizes his inability to play the same role long enough as a kind of ethical leprosy that can only destroy his friends. His decision to go to the terminal (the novel's last word) to keep his bargain after all indicates a final retreat from life.

The *No Exit* conclusiveness of *End of the Road* is slightly misleading in that Barth's next novel, *The Sot-Weed Factor*, carries forward motifs introduced in the antiphonal early works. But this third variation on the theme of innocence — Barth's as well as that of his characters — struck its initial readers as a radical departure. Not only was it in a surprisingly new mode, it also widened Barth's range spatially and temporally. Where the first two novels were parochially constrained within their twentieth-century Maryland locale, the historically reverberating, transoceanic *Sot-Weed Factor* charts the life of its hero, Ebenezer Cooke, in and around London, glances at his American birth, follows his enforced trip across the Atlantic to claim his father's Maryland estate and his wanderings after gulling himself out of it. *Floating Opera*, while implying the social density of its Eastern Shore microcosm, made do with a small cast of characters, and *End of the Road* was downright claustrophobic. The structural and characterological tightness, especially of the latter work, was the formal correlative for a confinement of minds in wandering mazes lost. In *Sot-Weed Factor* Barth loosens his form, conceivably in the hopes that temporal and spatial amplitude will permit his characters to burst their psychological and philosophical prisons.

What Barth perhaps means in the passage quoted earlier by being "mad at Flaubert . . . in a friendly way" is that he had come to feel the necessity for moving away from a tradition that *End of the Road* in part exemplifies — the novel as ordered, organic artifact where every mot juste creates its calibrated impact. The jeweled perfection of Jane Austen, Flaubert, and Joyce's *Dubliners* notwithstanding, for the later Barth the grounds of highest value in fiction are expansive grandeur, the wastefully panoramic sweep, a self-confident and even self-indulgent completeness. Both *Sot-Weed Factor* and *Giles* seek to recapture the boisterousness, the grandiose scale of Cervantes and Rabelais and the exuberant innocence of the English eighteenth-century novel. Todd Andrews had apologized that his Floating Opera was to be a baggy monster; in fact the pretense of random garrulousness conceals a carefully patterned narrative mosaic with a rigorously controlled point of view. Still, from Todd's intention to use a free form we can recognize the early appeal of the loose, open-ended structure for Barth (his desire to write a book with a plot "fancier than *Tom Jones*"), and *Sot-Weed Factor* is even more of a Floating Opera than the actual novel of that name. Its 756 pages in the 1967 hard-cover edition (trimmed from 806 in the 1960 edition) bulge with incident and character — it's a rambling, Gargantuan affair studded with absurd coincidences, with London tavern and bookseller scenes, with thinky exchanges embedded in excremental humor that throw into an ironic shade the "serious" encounters of Jake Horner and Joe Morgan; the book is asprawl with comic servants and Oxford dons, with poets and pirates and prostitutes, with Maryland tobacco growers and renegade Indians, with slaves and opium peddlers. Such furiousness of invention swirls out of the backwater intrigues of Maryland history, already complicated enough in the *Archives of Maryland*, but further muddied by Barth for thematic purposes: the labyrinthine obscurity, and ultimately the complete impenetrability, of seventeenth-century plot and counterplot conveys the difficulty of knowing the moral status of anything or anyone in the great world. The many rhetorical changes of pace reinforce Ebenezer's (and the reader's) epistemological quandary, for the novel ventriloquizes from one set piece to another — from fluent passages of Hudibrastic poetry to the Jacobean prose of John Smith's *Secret Historie*, from compressed disquisitions on historiography to interpolated short stories à la *Tom Jones*, from a fabliau with the same structure as Chaucer's *Reeve's Tale* to a six-page, bilingual cursing match in which a French and an English whore surely exhaust the metaphorical labels for their calling (a mock testimony to Barth's dazzlingly offhanded learning).

The "flabbergasting plot" in its veering precipitousness carries forward the trope of the road to suggest that, whatever the final disablement of Todd Andrews and Jake Horner, the fabular abilities of their creator are far from their terminal (though Barth seems to be hypersensitive to the possibilities of imaginative aridity). By widening and making more florid the terms of Todd's inquiry, Barth frames the philosophically naive "big" questions this time within the interstices of the historical novel, a maneuver that creates a variety of echo effects. The return to the burlesque mode of Sterne and Fielding allows for the unfettered expansiveness of the novel's youthful period; but onto that wide canvas Barth thrusts characters who, in the dialects of the late seventeenth century, are beset with ailments that *Floating Opera* and *End of the Road* tended (Laocoön notwithstanding) to define as primarily modern. The resulting comic suspension between two historical periods provides a breezily detached perspective upon the agonies of both, at the same time that it implies the venerable age of Barth's road.

Ebenezer Cooke, the gawky, taciturn young man who haunts London taverns in search of a vocation and, familiarly enough, an "identity," is not quite the youthful naif of the picaresque tradition. The recipient of an unusually comprehensive education from his gifted tutor, Henry Burlingame, Eben arbitrarily admires whomever he meets — "expert falconers, scholars, masons, chimneysweeps, prostitutes, admirals, catpurses, sailmakers, barmaids, apothecaries, and cannoneers alike." "Dizzy with the beauty of the possible" he throws up his hands at the task of choosing — whether notebook, a position on gambling, or a career. He is still a virgin at 28 because of a highly developed sense of mask, because he has never been single-minded enough to adopt a particular style of lovemaking. This habitual paralysis resolves itself in part when, as an undiscriminating admirer of *l'amour courtois*, scholastic metaphysics, and Neoplatonic idealism, he apotheosizes a London whore, Joan Toast, into a goddess of love. In such a transformation Barth rearranges the philosophical determinants that had been "split" between Jake and Joe in the previous novel: Eben's cosmopsis, once he deifies Joan, gives way to a polar exuberance in defense of his "essence" that reminds one of nothing so much as Joe's fanatical rationalism. The overblown mock-epic gusts of language with which Eben defends his virginity against this tart who rather enjoys her work typify his capacity to rhapsodize the most ungainly jetsam into something rare and beautiful: " 'Was't for gold that silver-footed Thetis shared the bed of Peleus, Achilles' sire? Think thee Venus and Anchises did their amorous work on consideration of five guineas? Nay, sweet Joan, a man seeks not in the market for the favors of a goddess!' "

Once he has discovered his calling as lover of Joan, Eben is led quite naturally to its twin, the vocation of the poet who will sing the praises of his sullied Beatrice. When his father, informed of his unproductive London life, orders him to cross the ocean to the family tobacco estate at Cooke's Point, Maryland, Eben includes within his apotheosis the jewel of the New World, Maryland itself. His overblown *Marylandiad*-to-be, as he describes it during an interview with Charles Calvert, Third Lord Baltimore (actually Henry Burlingame in one of his disguises), will be " 'an epic to out-epic epics: the history of the princely house of Charles Calvert, Lord Baltimore and Lord Proprietary of the Province of Maryland, relating the heroic founding of that province! The courage and perseverance of her settlers in battling barb'rous nature and fearsome salvage to wrest a territory from the wild and transform it to an earthly paradise! The majesty and enlightenment of her proprietors, who like kingly gardeners fostered the tender seeds of civilization in their rude soil, and so husbanded and cultivated them as to bring to fruit a Maryland beauteous beyond description; verdant, fertile, prosperous, and cultured; peopled with brave men and virtuous women, healthy, handsome, and refined: a Maryland, in short, splendid in her past, majestic in her present, and glorious in her future, the brightest jewel in the fair crown of England, owned and ruled to the benefit of both by a family second to none in the recorded history of the universal world — the whole done into heroic couplets, printed on linen, bound in calf, stamped in gold . . . and dedicated to Your Lordship!' "

The actuality of "beshitten Maryland" throws such lofty expectation into grotesque relief. Eben's chastity and poetic elevation are sorely tried by the intricate plots and all-pervasive scurviness of his voyage and misadventures in the New World. The history of Maryland is world history in small, "a string of plots, cabals, murthers, and machinations," a vortex of conspiracy within the larger whirlpool of late seventeenth-century colonial politics. From such actual historical personages as the several Lord Baltimores, Henry More, Isaac Newton, William Claiborne, and John Coode down to the lowliest besotted tobacco planter, all is bleared with comic sludge and smeared with excremental humor. For every imposing historical reputation there is a scurrilous "secret historie": the novel, for example, follows the sexual adventures of John Smith whose scatalogical career emerges from his journal entries scattered throughout the novel. All this is rendered with a circumstantial, enthusiastic mock realism. The tale's sheer length and the convolutions of plot and large cast of fools and knaves give the impression of heaviness — of the weight, the ubiquitousness, but also the attractiveness of the great world's power of corruption.

Inevitably, the gradual furnace of that world burns away Eben's illusions. His tobacco estate is an opium den and brothel; Joan

Toast's beauty, after she follows Eben to America, is irretrievably blasted by opium and syphilis; and *The Marylandiad* becomes not the panegyric that Eben had originally intended but *The Sot-Weed Factor*, a Hudibrastic satire filled with bitter misanthropy. Nevertheless, Eben retains the accouterments of his twin calling of epic poet and virgin long after experience has stripped him of belief, for he will not disavow his cardinal philosophical principle that there is a solidity to human character, an essence that no amount of disillusionment can alter.

Eben's opponent in this ancient debate about the one and the many is the "cosmophilist" Henry Burlingame, his friend and tutor who moves among the many professions of his life with gusto and a sure mastery. If Eben's continuing presence in the novel implies the stability of personality, Burlingame's discontinuous appearance as he threads his way among various disguises seriously challenges Eben's precarious sense of selfhood. Burlingame's America is itself an epistemological wilderness in which Eben wanders because of identities bestowed upon him by a traditional philosophical idealism and by his personal past — a father who insists that he take over the Maryland tobacco plantation. Conversely, Burlingame, an orphan who does not know his father, floats with consummate skill through a new world that is his proper metaphysical home. America's appeal for Burlingame is that it makes possible the shifting choice of identity: " 'There is a freedom there that's both a blessing and a curse. 'Tis more than just political and religious liberty — they come and go from one year to the next. 'Tis philosophic liberty I speak of, that comes from want of history. It makes every man an orphan like myself, that freedom, and can as well demoralize as elevate.' " Burlingame does not find the New World the Hell or Purgatorio that Eben comes to know, but "just a piece o' the great world like England — with the difference, haply, that the soil is vast and new where the sot-weed hath not drained it. What's

GERHARD JOSEPH

more, the reins and checks are few and weak; good plants and weeds alike grow tall." Burlingame pits such a capacity for pragmatic acceptance against Eben's "mystic ontological value," and the novel's many debates about the nature of history, of civilization, of man's position in the cosmos, of the appropriate life style for this poor forked animal sitting upon "a blind rock careening through space . . . rushing headlong to the grave" develop out of the dialectical confrontation of Eben's "innocence" and Burlingame's "experience."

The Sot-Weed Factor also explores more fully and consciously than the earlier novels the connection between identity and sexual knowledge. Eben's single-minded devotion to Joan Toast is now a cause, now an effect of his search for selfhood. But Barth interjects a post-Freudian motive into what Stendhal would have called such "crystallizations": Burlingame at one point suggests that it is Eben's sister, Anna, that Eben really loves. The idealization of Joan Toast projects a passion for his sister upon an acceptable woman, and his insistence upon chastity makes it possible for him to avoid a carnal commitment to any woman other than his sister. The perverse element in Eben's innocence finds its mirror reversal in Burlingame's perverse doctrine of experience. Burlingame is anxious to take on sexually all comers — women, men, and, in one of the novel's more hilarious chapters, pigs. It is with typical tongue-in-cheek hyperbole that he proclaims his catholic sexual tastes to Eben: " 'I love the world, sir, and so make love to it! I have sown my seed in men and women, in a dozen sorts of beasts, in the barky boles of trees and the honeyed wombs of flowers; I have dallied on the black breast of the earth, and clipped her fast; I have wooed the waves of the sea, impregnated the four winds, and flung my passion skywards to the stars!' "

The *ménage à trois* of the first two novels receives a further turn of the screw from this juxtaposition of Eben's virginity and Burlingame's pan-sexualism. The incestuous bond between Eben and Anna is complicated by Burlingame's love of them both or, more accurately, of their twinhood (he defends that love to Eben by means of a learned historical survey of geminology). Barth here makes explicit what had been a subterranean motif of his earlier work — the degree to which the *ménage à trois* offers the novelist an opportunity to explore the competing homosexual and hetero-sexual impulses in man. The multiple sexual confusions do more or less straighten themselves out by novel's end in a traditional enough way: Eben, who comes fully to realize the destructive effects of his platonizing on himself and on others, does marry and bed the opium-addicted, syphilitic Joan Toast; and Burlingame's promis-cuity, an extension of his belief in a New World philosophical free-dom, is revealed to cover a sexual impotence that he cannot cure until his "search for the father" is successful. Only when he can come to a conventional awareness of a limited self does he get his beloved Anna with child. To be sure, this symmetrical comedic straightening out of lovers is blurred in the novel's final chapter by Joan Toast's death in childbirth and Burlingame's disappearance for good among the Indians, whereupon the twins are plagued by their old suspicions of incestuous feelings as together they bring up Anna's child. But by and large the mask of the eighteenth-century picaresque mode which looks back to the ancient patterns of New Comedy (in both of which the possibility of incest operated as a stock comic obstacle) serves to dilute any "serious" conclusion.

As *Sot-Weed Factor* and the *Giles* to follow suggest, a degree of emotional flatness is the price that the parodist agrees to pay for his knowledgeable artificiality and mannered thoroughness. Whether in his depletion of the picaresque mode, in his erudite catalogues of ideas, or in his name-calling contest between the prostitutes, Barth tries to convey the impression that sheer exhaustiveness for its own sake contributes to a meaningful comic order. The longer and more contrived the shaggy-dog fiction, the better. But because of Barth's intellectual passion for following a literary genre, a philosophical assumption, or a linguistic pattern to the absolute end of its road, his characters frequently do not have much emotional depth. Aware of the ancient resonances of his hero's experience, Barth can wittily and with considerable rhetorical gusto explore the meaning of the archetype. But insisting upon a mock-epic distance, Barth only rarely enters, and lets his reader enter, fully into his character's suffering and loss. For the most part he writes "novels which imitate the form of the Novel, by an author who imitates the role of Author."

Of course, as he has noted, this sense of being at several removes from reality is nothing new for the novel — "it's about where the genre began, with *Quixote* imitating *Amadis of Gaul*, Cervantes pretending to be the Cid Hamete Benengeli (and Alonzo Quijano pretending to be Don Quixote), or Fielding parodying Richardson." Eben's defense of his virginity which echoes that of Joseph Andrews which in turn parodies that of Pamela, etc., creates the *regressus in infinitum* effect that Barth admires in the fictions of Nabokov and Borges, the literary funhouse in which the reader is invited to amuse himself. But Barth's characters, interesting as they are, cannot possess the achieved sense of clearly observed humanity, the degree of characterological "originality," that one feels in the great characters of realistic fiction or even in the parodic characters of the early novel. For the further the regression from the pre-existing archetype, the more surely a character becomes a learned and witty commentary upon the archetype, a pale fire indeed. Like Nabokov and Borges, then, Barth tries in his most recent work to make a virtue of the necessity of parody and self-parody: to create original works of art out of the certainty that at this late date in the history of Western narrative, it is impossible to write original narratives.

30

Though Ebenezer Cooke and Henry Burlingame obviously combine to echo the traditional hero of Western literature in manifold ways, Barth was apparently not aware of *Sot-Weed Factor*'s comprehensively paradigmatic design until he happened, after its publication, to read Lord Raglan's *The Hero*. Raglan's work establishes the pattern of mythic heroism by abstracting from the lives of the world's culture heroes a list of twenty-two characteristics and then "grading" representative heroes according to the number of characteristics they possess. Barth was struck by the fact that Cooke and Burlingame taken together (as they might be) do almost as well by Raglan's standards as Oedipus (who fulfills twenty-one of the twenty-two prerequisites — "there's always one smart guy in the class who messes up the curve"). Out of a subsequent absorption in modern mythographers and comparative religionists — Otto Rank, Joseph Campbell, Jung, Frazer, Freud (whatever came to hand) — Barth apparently set out in his next novel to create a parable of mythic heroism with a controlled relentlessness and an exactitude that went beyond the accidental typicality of *Sot-Weed Factor*. If the implied moral allegory of Eben's pilgrimage through life is frequently swamped by the rich detail of Maryland history, *Giles* accentuates its allegory with deliberate artifice, annotating the meaning of each step that its hero takes in his cyclical adventure from mysterious birth, through rites of passage, to his momentary illumination at the womb of things, through the mature period of lawgiving to his civilization, and toward an extraordinary sacrificial death.

The formal educational experience that had at times been peripheral and muted in earlier novels becomes the radical trope of *Giles*, a *Bildungsroman ad absurdum*. After some Nabokov-like publisher's disclaimers describing the editorial vicissitudes of this highly controversial manuscript and a "cover letter" to the editors and publishers by "J. B." describing how the text came into his

31

hands, the fable proper assumes the form of the Revised New Syllabus, a sacred computer tape chronicle of the life and teachings of
George Giles, the Grand Tutor of New Tammany College, as
spoken by George himself, prepared by the West Campus Automatic Computer (WESCAC) from several texts fed into it by
George's son and disciple, and given to the public in its present
form by Barth, a recent convert to Gilesianism. (Such a playful re-
fraction of the author's vision into written, spoken, and mechanical
"voices" from several problematical sources — Barth's latest state-
ment of man's epistemological dilemma — will receive its most
technical elaboration in *Lost in the Funhouse*.) Rescued from the
tapelift of WESCAC after a mysterious birth, the narrator is reared
as Billy Bocksfuss, the Ag-Hill Goat-Boy, by Max Spielman, an
outcast professor with a fondness for the company of goats. The
naive goat-boy gradually discovers that he is more human being
than goat, and, journeying forth from his caprine Eden after having killed a brother goat, he bids farewell to his "hornless goat-
hood" and strikes out, "a horned human student," for Commence-
ment Gate. But his progress across the Great Mall is no ordinary
one, for he takes upon himself the profession of the hero who will
in his time save all of studentdom. The form of his quest will be the
entrance into the belly of WESCAC to change its AIM (Automatic
Implementation Mechanism) which threatens to destroy the entire
student body. And as George learns, he is peculiarly suited to this
task in that he is himself GILES (the Grand Tutorial Ideal, Labora-
tory Specimen), son of WESCAC and a human mother.

The novel thus becomes a hybrid of genres: part sacred book,
animal fable, science-fiction fantasy, political allegory, educational
satire, epic, and what not else, the work has so exasperated some reviewers that they have been unable to see in it more than an ingen-
iously prolonged put-on that self-indulgently stitches together the
shreds and patches of Barth's learning. As it insinuates with wild

incongruity the jargon of computer technology into the combined structures of contemporary politics and ancient myth, the reader is engulfed, as Richard Poirier has protested, "with the wastes of time, with cultural shards and rubbish."

But what is most striking about Barth's alternative to the real world is the ultimate seriousness of the gigantic hoax, the *lacrimae rerum* that the comic audaciousness only partly conceals. Furthermore, whether hoax or not, the encyclopedic range and vastly complex order of this reinvention of the world are mightily impressive. Giles Goat-Boy — the very name in its amalgamation of the mechanical, animal, and strictly human aspects of man's destiny encapsulates the novel's illustration of Spielman's Law, that ontogeny recapitulates cosmogeny. "My day, my year, my life, and the history of West Campus," the hero learns, "are wheels within wheels." As George advances toward his moment of illumination, rewinding the very tape of time, his ritual return to WESCAC's belly becomes a compendium of human history, ancient and contemporary. Heroes and Grand Tutors of the ages— Christ, Buddha, Moses, Socrates, Oedipus, Aeneas, Dante — illuminate or baffle George with the examples of their earlier journeys. George must at the same time define his local quest against the backdrop of recent political events, for it takes place during the Quiet Riot between East and West Campus just after Campus Riot II. The goat-boy has thinly veiled versions of Eisenhower, John and Jacqueline Kennedy, and Khrushchev to contend with while he tries as part of his initial assignment to resolve the boundary dispute between East and West Campus. The humorous richness of such characters usually arises from a clash between their allegorical significances and certain bizarre, usually sexual, personal quirks.

To isolate a figure whose make-up indicates Barth's method, Max Spielman is driven by psychosexual cravings that are the animal foundations for the "higher" political and philosophical meanings of his character — Barth will insist upon a like ontological continuum for every one of his characters. Because he is a professor of Mathematical Psycho-Proctology interested in getting to the bottom of things — his masterwork is *The Riddle of the Sphincters* — he is content to spend his time among goats where he can fully indulge his interest in nether regions. The "father of WESCAC" who has taught the computer how to EAT all of studentdom, he has been exiled to the Ag-Hill goat farm during the wizard hunts of the Quiet Riot; in the vaudeville-stage German accent with which he utters his ambivalent profundities ("'Der goats is humaner than der men, und der men is goatisher than der goats'") he refers vaguely to J. Robert Oppenheimer, just as his arch-opponent, Dr. Eblis Eierkopf, has some momentary connections with Edward Teller. At his most archetypal Spielman becomes the Eternally Suffering and Wandering Jew, as well as the "helper" who prepares the hero for the return to the *Axis Mundi* of his birth so that he may acquire the wisdom to carry history forward.

In the past and at its most successful allegory has made such centrifugation of character as seamless as possible, and readers have legitimately been disturbed by failures of integration and serious inconsistencies of denotation. The primary way in which Barth parodies the traditional techniques of allegory is to jump with tonal and thematic abandon among the various referents of his allegory in the recognition that "you don't have to explain a myth at all these days. . . . what you do is to look for correspondences, merely, between it and other things, and correspondences of course may be manifold, coexistent, and equally 'legitimate,' though of unequal interest and heuristic value." The "meaning" of any character is the integrated totality of his roles (a Burlingame thesis), just as the meaning of Giles' tale of heroism is the sum of its correspondences. Whatever the quality of *Giles*, its size is thus as necessary as the size of such other literary cosmologies as *Para-*

dise Lost and the *Divine Comedy.* Its ritual motions are as comprehensively allusive, and the characters who move into the goat-boy's purview as loaded with historical, philosophical, and sociological significance, as the synthesizing imagination of a mock-cosmologist can manage. Anastasia, the innocently promiscuous eternal woman with whom George finds his moment of illumination within WESCAC; Pete Greene, the prototypical American (Huck Finn, Will Rogers, George Babbitt rolled into one), and his castrating wife, Sally Anne; Maurice Stoker, the diabolical Dean o' Flunks and controller of the West Campus Power Station who is related to and cynically corrupts many of the novel's more respectable characters — such figures keep shifting their ethical and emotional shape as correspondence is piled upon correspondence in West Campus' spectral landscape.

Still, most of the characters are relatively easy for the goat-boy to understand since the meanings they simultaneously or sequentially embody tend to have a common ideological center. The true Burlingame of the novel, a configuration of elliptical poses who continually defies the goat-boy's attempts at comprehension, is Harold Bray. A false Grand Tutor, a mocking anti-Giles, Bray now anticipates, now shadows the tragic pattern of George's pilgrimage. Against a Western conception of tragedy, he flaunts a malign transcendental mystery; against George's serious vocation as Grand Tutor, he pits a talent for metaphysical mockery as he shifts from pose to pose; against George's hard-won integrity, he brays forth his magical proliferation into the many.

This familiar question of whether unity or multiplicity is the primary tendency of existence poses itself anew as the theme of optical difficulty. George is provided with *the* exemplary model for his own journey toward self-knowledge during a theatrical performance: *Taliped Decanus*, a forty-seven-page, scene-by-scene recasting of *Oedipus Rex* in contemporary doggerel, which describes the fall of the Dean of Cadmus College "who'll go to any lengths for answers" and who blinds himself when he discovers his ancient crime. The novel's other optical sideshows that spin off from this root burlesque (Pete Greene, for instance, accidentally puts out his eye in a funhouse) and the different mirrors and lenses pressed upon George as phenomenological aids all point to the difficulty of "seeing," of knowing whether the essential cognitive act in judging one's fellow beings and the great world is discrimination or synthesis.

Thus the key to asserting control over WESCAC is the understanding of the assignment to "Pass All Fail All," the cryptic circular message which WESCAC had imprinted upon George's Pre-Natal Aptitude Test card and which is repeated at the time of his matriculation. As George performs his initial labors he discovers and systematically applies the principle of analysis, distinguishing "Tick from Tock, East Campus from West Campus, Grand Tutor from goat, appearance from reality" and, climactically, Passage from Failure. When such sharpening of definition produces the worst kind of chaos, George commits himself to its opposite, a union of contraries, which is no more of an answer. Finally in a transcendence of categories by which an awareness of body and soul, male and female, passing and failing is triumphantly obliterated, the goat-boy and Anastasia sexually joined to one another make their way through WESCAC's belly satisfied to "feel a way through the contradictions" of this life, to accept on ecstatic faith "the seamless University" that "knew aught of . . . distinctions." From the sexual loathing of Todd Andrews and Jake Horner through Ebenezer's reluctant intercourse with this world as syphilitic whore, Barth moves to the goat-boy's lyrical sexual embrace of the cosmos, even if it be a cosmos of Barth's making.

And yet the goat-boy's blinding insight is at best a momentary affirmation. In the Revised New Syllabus' posttape (possibly spurious, of course) George toward the end of his life views with plangent weariness the steady distortion of his gospel, and the Grand Tutor's momentary triumph is placed within the larger context of the tragic hero's inevitable loss. All of his way stations have merely been preparation for an ultimate futility: "the pans remain balanced for better and worse . . . Nay, rather, for worse, always for worse. Late or soon, we lose. Sudden or slow, we lose. The bank exacts its charge for each redistribution of our funds. There is an entropy to time, a tax on change: four nickels for two dimes, but always less silver; our books stay reconciled, but who in modern terms can tell heads from tails?"

Such slang-drenched lyricism never quite loses its undercurrent of self-mockery; the novel's many flashes of wit and genius as well as its longueurs are grounded in a self-reductive circumspection. But by journey's end the parodic mode has become a melancholy instrument indeed. The final effect of *Giles* is precisely one of controlled hovering — among intellectual oppositions, mythic correspondences, and literary attitudes. It is undoubtedly infuriating in its obsessive insistence upon filling in every nook of its closed system while admitting in a self-deprecation Dante or Milton would never have imagined that the vast metaphor is something of a joke. The fit audience willing to sit through to the end of the cosmic joke has apparently been small. But for the reader who can admire the hit-and-miss audacity of the system, who can shrug off the heavy-handed and follow with delight the witty play of correspondence, and who will imaginatively enter into the spirit of the goat-boy's deepening vision, the impression of facile ingenuity gradually gives way to one of moving earnestness. As for the quality of that vision, the critical response to *Giles* merely illustrates the truism that in all but the very greatest novels of ideas one reader's imaginative profundity is another's puerile shallowness and irresponsible navel-gazing. On the whole, the life-and-death game seems to this reader well worth the candle.

While alluding sympathetically, in an essay on Borges, to a putative remark of Saul Bellow's that to be technically up to date is the least important attribute of a writer, Barth adds that this least important attribute may nevertheless be essential. The writer must, he feels, pay attention to the innovations of the best of his contemporaries — he singles out Beckett, Nabokov, and Borges for himself — for he can and does learn from them even when he does not directly imitate. Barth's most recent book, *Lost in the Funhouse*, provides ample evidence that, aside from all questions of aesthetic success, he is one of the two or three most aware, most technically experimental writers of acknowledged power at work in America today.

This collection of short pieces, most of which were published separately from 1963 to 1968, complicates his urge to blur received discriminations among genre by attacking the traditional expectation of fiction as the printed word. Of the fourteen fictions only a few are designed expressly for print, others are meant for live voice — either authorial or non-authorial — or tape, still others for various combinations of those media. "Title," as Barth describes the most versatile of the lot, "makes somewhat separate but equally valid senses, in several media: print, monophonic recorded authorial voice, stereophonic ditto in dialogue with itself, live authorial voice, live ditto in dialogue with monophonic ditto aforementioned, and live ditto interlocutory with stereophonic et cetera, my own preference." (A recent *Esquire* piece, "Help," actually provides a musical score to show how such verbal counterpointing will look on the printed page.) As Giles compressed within himself the continuum of the race from primitive animal to autonomous computer, so Barth is working in these latest intermediary experiments toward a recapitulation of fictional expression from oral through printed to electronic means.

The earliest written pieces take the print medium for granted while the later ones become more and more experimentally intermediary. And just as Barth's novels move from Maryland-based verisimilitude through historical fable to mythic allegory, so do these stories follow a like pattern. Several of the early, frankly autobiographical "Ambrose" stories set on the Eastern Shore detail with a conventional realism a young boy's search for a name and an identity. "Ambrose His Mark" recounts the bizarre incident which led to the "naming" of the child and the resultant strangeness with which his ego thereafter contemplated its sign. In "Water-Message" this same child's voyeuristic initiation into sexuality is incomprehensible until he experiences a "greater vision, vague and splendrous," in the form of a bottle at the seashore with an all but empty piece of paper in it, a messenger from the universe that sends him an intimation of its meaning. His macroscopic insight is matched in the story's final lines with a new microscopic precision as well, for he notices that "those shiny bits in the paper's texture were splinters of wood pulp. Often as he'd seen them in the leaves of cheap tablets, he had not thitherto embraced that fact." The optical strangeness of Ambrose receives its climactic treatment in the volume's title story, "Lost in the Funhouse," which describes a family outing to Ocean City, his adolescent erotic fantasies about a young neighbor along on the trip, and the deterioration of a coherent sense of self while wandering through the funhouse mirror room in which he unaccountably finds himself. The funhouse becomes the excruciatingly self-conscious symbol for the many distorted perspectives from which he views his troubled psyche, a barely disguised reflection of the authorial narrator's own disintegrating self. The fictional technique verbally duplicates the endless replication of images in a funhouse mirror, meandering with an artful lack of control between the point of view of Ambrose in various guises and a self-chastising narrator lost within his own story. As the narrator interrupts his tale with literary and linguistic exegesis of the most obsessive sort, we have instead of the tight structure of the first two Ambrose stories a monstrous plot that "doesn't rise by meaningful steps but winds upon itself, digresses, retreats, hesitates, sighs, collapses, expires." And as Ambrose accepts his lifelong entrapment within a labyrinth of his mind's making, he merges with the amazed narrator to provide a rationale for the entire volume: "He wishes he had never entered the funhouse. But he has. Then he wishes he were dead. But he's not. Therefore he will construct funhouses for others and be their secret operator — though he would rather be among the lovers for whom funhouses are designed."

Some of the chambers in Barth's funhouse are merely that — self-contained inventions into which the author has stumbled as if by mistake, metaphorical playground for his habitual themes. In "Petition" Body and Soul are conceived of as feuding Siamese twins, with Soul having to put up with gross indignities because his belly is fastened to the small of Body's back. In a marvelous echo of Barth's earlier love triangles, both twins — the anterior profanely, the posterior sacredly — are in love with the same pretty contortionist and the three earn their living by an act billed as The Eternal Triangle. (The funhouse is, after all, a place of amusement, no matter how desperate the wanderer.) The bizarre psychomachy takes the form of a petition addressed by Soul to a Siamese potentate visiting White Plains, New York, asking that he arrange the surgical separation of the mismatched brothers. In words recalling the epistemological vacillations of the novels, the eloquent brother concludes his plea with a Barthian *cri de coeur*: "To be one: paradise! To be two: bliss! But to be both and neither is unspeakable."

These fabular concoctions transcend the time and space of the

Ambrose stories and exist entirely within a chosen metaphor whose ambivalent implications a speaker, entrapped within its aesthetic context, explores. "Night-Sea Journey" transforms the Barthian "road" into a conceivably endless and purposeless swim by a speaker who gradually reveals himself to be a philosophically sophisticated sperm toward a shore (the ovum? — at any rate, a goal eventually postulated as "She"), the doubtful union of swimmer and shore overseen by a Maker who is just as problematic. The influence of Borges seems especially clear in the brevity and attenuation of these fictions. Although they seem informed by the same creative principle of metaphorical elaboration as *Giles*, they lack its purposeful exhaustiveness. In each of the chambers within the larger funhouse, a single voice momentarily struggles with its metaphor to be replaced a few pages or a tape later by another voice. The most puzzled voices of all are those of the author himself in "Autobiography," "Title," and "Life-Story" trying to get a story told, a plot going — all unsuccessfully and with a maximum of fierce self-loathing ("Another story about a writer writing a story! Another regressus in infinitum! Who doesn't prefer art that at least overtly imitates something other than its own processes?").

What emerges powerfully from this wildly reverberating volume is a sure sense of voice, of the modulated resonances that these echo chambers take from one another. The optical confusions uniting the Ambrose stories and focused most explicitly in the funhouse mirror trope give way in Barth's recent, most experimental fiction to aural distortion as the proper trope for man's metaphysical puzzlement. And Barth has always had a better ear than eye — his work is relatively bare in landscape and visual detail, but he has the ventriloquist's gift of parodying voices, especially lyrical voices, out of the literary past. The two most interesting pieces in the volume, "Echo" and "Menelaiad," demonstrate clearly the aural direction in which Barth is moving.

If narrative originality is impossible for the modern artist, if he accepts his fate as parodic translator and annotator of pre-existing archetypes, what can still be original is the unique source of the voice, the authorial instrument that shapes the retelling. "Echo," a monologue describing Narcissus' attempt to escape Echo by seeking advice from Tiresias in the prophet's cave, accomplishes the complete amalgamation of the first- and third-person point of view. Narcissus seems to be the speaker, telling his familiar tale in the third person to Tiresias as an antidote to self-love: "One does well," the story opens, "to speak in the third person, the seer advises, in the manner of Theban Tiresias. A cure for self-absorption is saturation: telling the story over as though it were another's until like a much-repeated word it loses sense." As Narcissus explores this perspective, lapsing at one point into the first person within the first person, we are led to suspect that the speaker may be either Tiresias or Echo, in which case the identity of the interlocutor is just as doubtful. While the narrative line is relatively clear because of the myth's familiarity, it becomes impossible for everyone involved to distinguish teller from listener and, ultimately, narrative from narrator. For the point of the myth is precisely the "autognostic verge" on which all three of the characters interchangeably live (with the author and reader).

Barth's op fictions thus explore visual and aural distinctions to dramatize an endlessly refracting and reverberating reality. But this insight is a dangerous one for the artist, who finds it increasingly difficult to maintain any aesthetic distance from his creations. Human character, including his own, becomes for him a series of Chinese boxes, each one containing a different version of itself in an infinite aural regression. The epitome of this entrapment within a fabular *regressus in infinitum* is also the volume's longest fiction, "Menelaiad." In this slangy, wisecracking redaction of Book IV of *The Odyssey* Menelaus attempts to wrest from Proteus on the beach at Pharos the gift of immortality, the secret of Helen's love after her return from Troy. Menelaus must hold fast to the slippery god as he shifts identity from beast to beast, object to object, person to person. The difficulty of the task is formally caught as Menelaus peels away the layers of voices that constitute his tangled point of view. At the very center of his "ravelled fabrication" the reader is at a seventh remove from the outer voice ("' " ' " ' " in print) as Menelaus imagines his own voice telling Telemachus and Peisistratus of imagining Helen hearing Proteus hearing Eiodethea (Proteus' daughter) hearing Menelaus (critic within critic!) describing the fall of Troy and the repossession of Helen. Only by exhausting the guises that reality can take may he fable back to the single identity from which he began, that single voice which "yarns on through everything to itself"; only at the end of his rhetorical tether can he accept "Proteus's terrifying last disguise, Beauty's spouse's odd Elysium: the absurd, unending possibility" that Helen has always loved him and only him.

Such mind-boggling acrobatics as Menelaus' attempt to "hold on" to something — a beloved, a god, an audience — intimate a desperation which must in some sense be autobiographical. Authorial experiments like "Life-Story," after all, enclose such painfully playful admissions as the fact that "while he did not draw his characters and situations directly from life nor permit his author-protagonist to do so, any moderately attentive reader of his oeuvre, his what, could infer for example that its author feared for example schizophrenia, impotence creative and sexual, suicide — in short living and dying." More important than any personal difficulties is Barth's awareness that he is working within an "apocalyptic ambience" to create a "literature of exhausted possibility" at a time when the novel, if not the printed word altogether, is in its last stages of depletion. It is then the conjunction of a personal and a literary ultimacy, both passionately felt, that accounts for the baroque style and the increasingly involuted experiments of *Lost in the Funhouse*. To be sure, one occasionally feels in this work as in earlier ones that the advertised awareness of literary ultimacy acts as too self-indulgent a mask, as too uncontrolled a rationalization for the author's psychic dislocations.

But those reviewers who have read the volume as a dead end from which no forward progress is possible have perhaps underestimated the resourcefulness of the fabulist's endgame. Scheherazade, Barth's *avant-gardiste*, must unfortunately court the disaster of silence. (Barth has remarked of two authors relevant to his own situation that Borges is blind and Beckett is approaching virtual muteness.) Her perilous balance between fantasy and reality is not a chosen condition but one forced upon her by the need to confront her odd situation intelligently. And that is a meaningful way for her to confront her "times" as well, although the indirection of fable will always strike some readers as an evasion of the Real World. As one contemplates the cheerful ingenuity of her stratagems to avoid the creative impotence that will mean her death, one realizes that her sentence while a source of terror gradually becomes the necessary and even the conventional goad for her fables. A thousand and one fictions would, no doubt, be a decent output for any lifetime.

↗ Selected Bibliography

Works of John Barth

"Lilith and the Lion," *Hopkins Review*, 4:49–53 (Fall 1950).

The Floating Opera. New York: Appleton-Century-Crofts, 1956; revised edition, New York: Doubleday, 1967.

The End of the Road. New York: Doubleday, 1958; revised edition, 1967.

"Landscape: The Eastern Shore," *Kenyon Review*, 22:104–10 (Winter 1960).

The Sot-Weed Factor. New York: Doubleday, 1960; revised edition, 1967.

"My Two Muses," *Johns Hopkins Magazine*, 12:9–13 (April 1961).

"Mystery and Tragedy: The Two Motions of Ritual Heroism," unpublished lecture given at State University of New York at Geneseo, December 10, 1964.

Giles Goat-Boy. New York: Doubleday, 1966.

"The Literature of Exhaustion," *Atlantic Monthly*, 220:29–34 (August 1967); reprinted in *The American Novel since World War II*, edited by Marcus Klein. New York: Fawcett Publications, 1969. Pp. 267–79.

Lost in the Funhouse. New York: Doubleday, 1968.

"Help," *Esquire*, 77:108–9 (September 1969).

Current American Reprints

The End of the Road. New York: Avon. $.75. New York: Bantam. $.95.

The Floating Opera. New York: Avon. $.75.

Giles Goat-Boy. New York: Fawcett World Library. $1.25.

Lost in the Funhouse. New York: Bantam. $.95.

The Sot-Weed Factor. New York: Universal Library. $1.50. New York: Bantam. $1.25.

Bibliography

Bryer, Jackson R. "Two Bibliographies" (Barth and John Hawkes), *Critique*, 6:86–89 (Fall 1963).

Critical Studies

Bluestone, George. "John Wain and John Barth: The Angry and the Accurate," *Massachusetts Review*, 1:582–89 (May 1960).

GERHARD JOSEPH

Bradbury, John M. "Absurd Insurrection: The Barth-Percy Affair," *South Atlantic Quarterly*, 68:319–29 (Summer 1969).

Diser, Philip E. "The Historical Ebenezer Cooke," *Critique*, 10:48–59 (1968).

Enck, John. "John Barth: An Interview," *Wisconsin Studies in Contemporary Literature*, 6:3–14 (Winter–Spring 1965).

Fiedler, Leslie A. "John Barth: An Eccentric Genius," *New Leader*, 44:22–24 (February 13, 1961).

———. *The Return of the Vanishing American*. New York: Stein and Day, 1968.

Garis, Robert. "Whatever Happened to John Barth?" *Commentary*, 42:89–95 (October 1966).

Holder, Alan. " 'What Marvelous Plot . . . Was Afoot?' History in Barth's *The Sot-Weed Factor*," *American Quarterly*, 20:596–604 (Fall 1968).

Hyman, Stanley Edgar. "John Barth's First Novel," *New Leader*, 48:20–21 (April 12, 1965).

Kerner, David. "Psychodrama in Eden," *Chicago Review*, 13:59–67 (Winter–Spring 1959).

Kiely, Benedict, "Ripeness Was Not All: John Barth's *Giles Goat-Boy*," *Hollins Critic*, 3:1–12 (1966).

Knapp, Edgar H. "Found in the Barthhouse: Novelist as Savior," *Modern Fiction Studies*, 14:446–51 (Winter 1968–69).

Miller, Russell H. "*The Sot-Weed Factor*: A Contemporary Mock-Epic," *Critique*, 8:88–100 (Winter 1965–66).

Noland, Richard W. "John Barth and the Novel of Comic Nihilism," *Wisconsin Studies in Contemporary Literature*, 7:239–57 (Autumn 1966).

Poirier, Richard. "The Politics of Self-Parody," *Partisan Review*, 35:339–53 (Summer 1968).

Rovit, Earl. "The Novel as Parody: John Barth," *Critique*, 6:77–85 (Fall 1963).

Samuels, Charles T. "John Barth: A Buoyant Denial of Relevance," *Commonweal*, 85:80–82 (October 21, 1966).

Schickel, Richard. "*The Floating Opera*," *Critique*, 6:53–67 (Fall 1963).

Scholes, Robert. *The Fabulators*. New York: Oxford University Press, 1967

Smith, Herbert. "Barth's Endless Road," *Critique*, 6:68–76 (Fall 1963).

Stubbs, John C. "John Barth as Novelist of Ideas: The Themes of Value and Identity," *Critique*, 8:101–16 (Winter 1965).

Tanner, Tony. "The Hoax That Joke Built," *Partisan Review*, 34:102–9 (Winter 1967).

———. "No Exit," *Partisan Review*, 36:293–99 (Number 2, 1969).

Tractenberg, Alan. "Barth and Hawkes: Two Fabulists," *Critique*, 6:4–18 (Fall 1963).

46